ISSUE NO. 10   EMMETT MAGAZINE   OCTOBER 2024

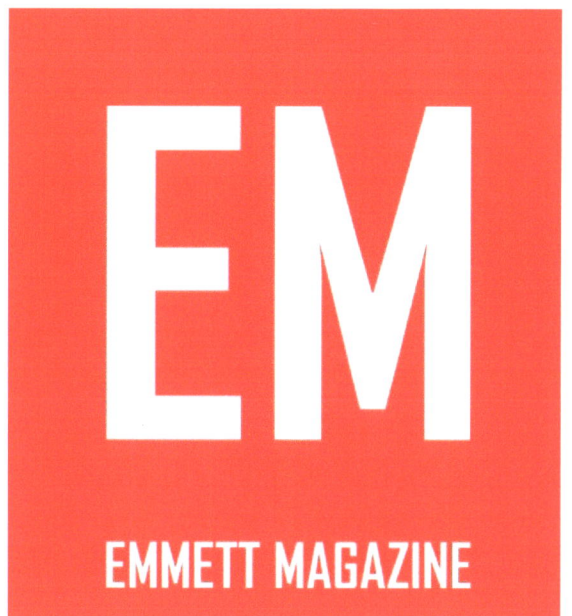

OCTOBER ISSUE 2024

DONALD PARTLOW

PIECES OF ME

SOLO EXHIBITION

THE BLACK GENIUS ART SHOW

PHOTOGRRAPHY

PAGES 2-32

EXHIBITION COURTESY PHOTOS

EMMETT PUBLISHING

©EMMETT MAGAZINE 2024. ALL RIGHTS RESERVED.

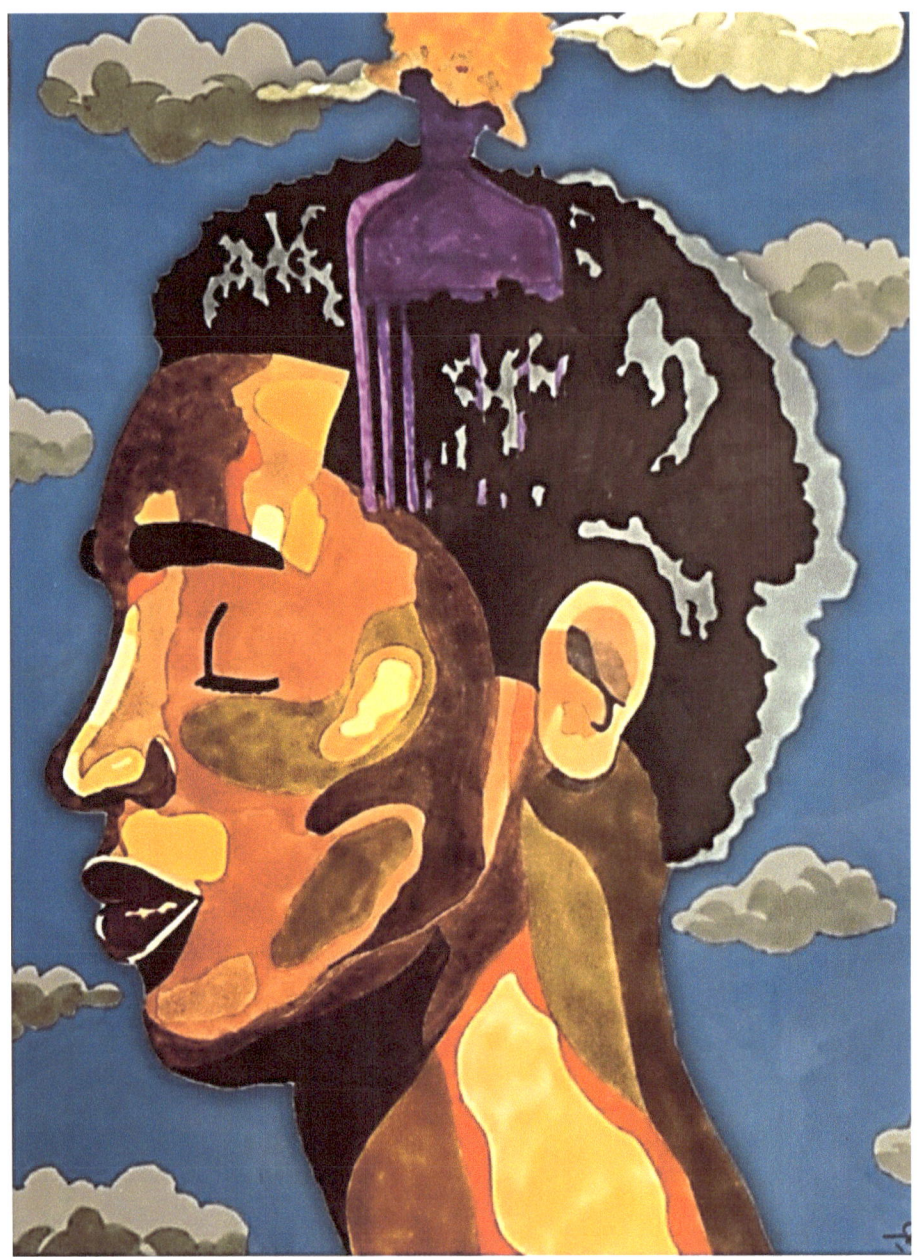

Donald Partlow: Biography

By Emmett Williams

Donald Partlow is an accomplished comic art illustrator and jazz art illustrator, known for his evocative depictions of iconic jazz legends such as Miles Davis, Nina Simone, and Marvin Gaye. His artwork, deeply rooted in both the comic and jazz worlds, beautifully captures the essence of each subject, blending vibrant storytelling with emotive visual interpretations. His artistic journey, a testament to both passion and perseverance, has been highlighted in prominent publications like *Emmett Magazine*, which showcases artists, models, fashion designers, actors, and entertainers.

Born in Baltimore, Maryland, in the mid-sixties, Donald has spent most of his life in his home state, except for the time he served in the U.S. Air Force. His early creative influences came from his mother, a dedicated Baltimore City Public School teacher, who encouraged him to channel his imagination into art. Together, they would collaborate on seasonal and holiday bulletin boards at the schools where she taught, sparking Donald's love for artistic expression.

Donald's passion for art began with comic books, particularly Spider-Man. He related to Peter Parker, the geeky, nerdy kid behind the mask, which fueled his desire to create characters of his own—characters with powers that allowed them to be "cool" and fit in. His fascination with comic art was the foundation of his creative career, and over the years, Donald has designed and developed numerous original characters.

Donald received his formal training in Graphic Arts at Mergenthaler Vocational Technical High School. After graduation, he joined the U.S. Air Force, but his artistic journey took an unexpected turn at the age of 32 when he was diagnosed with Relapsing Multiple Sclerosis. The disease temporarily robbed him of his vision, left him reliant on a cane and walker, and led doctors to predict he would be wheelchair-bound by age 36. The MS eventually went into remission, but it left Donald with permanent nerve and sensory damage in his hands, which led him to stop creating art for a time.

In December 2021, Donald experienced a pivotal moment in his life when he reconnected with a high school friend, Aaron, who encouraged him to pick up a pencil and start drawing again. With Aaron's support and practical tips, such as using harder lead pencils for lighter sketching and art markers to improve his grip and control, Donald found his way back to art. Since then, he hasn't stopped creating, reigniting his passion and honing his craft.

Donald primarily works in mixed media, employing oil and acrylic-based art markers, ink, and watercolors. His style has evolved into a fusion of comic art and jazz illustration, capturing the dynamic energy of both mediums. His artistic depictions of jazz greats like Miles Davis, Nina Simone, and Marvin Gaye blend the improvisational spirit of jazz with the vibrant aesthetic of comic books, creating a unique and compelling visual experience.

Donald's work has gained notable attention. He has been featured in multiple issues of *Emmett Magazine* (November 2022, December 2022, and July 2024), which are available through Amazon, Barnes & Noble, and other outlets. His art has also been showcased at various events, including The Holiday Makers Market at Baltimore's Harborplace and the Baltimore City-sponsored "Art After Dark" live event. In addition, Donald is a resident artist at "The Black Genius Art

Show" held at Genius Guice Studios, where his works are celebrated for their depth and emotional resonance.

Currently, Donald is presenting his first solo exhibition, titled *Pieces of Me*, which runs throughout October 2024. This featured artist showcase is a personal reflection of his creative journey, revealing the intimate and profound connection he shares with his subjects, as well as his ability to channel both triumph and adversity into his art.

Donald also maintains an active presence on Instagram under the handle @dpartlow2, where he documents his artistic evolution and shares his latest creations with a growing community of art lovers and supporters. Since January 2022, his account has become a platform for engaging with followers, offering a behind-the-scenes look at his creative process, and showcasing his ongoing journey as an artist.

About the Artist

Emmett Magazine has been a significant platform for showcasing Donald Partlow's work since 2022. In sharing his personal story, Donald embodies one of the key values of the magazine: overcoming adversity through sheer willpower and creative expression. Emmett Ardle Williams, the magazine's founder, has always believed in telling the stories of individuals who triumph over life's challenges, and Donald's narrative of battling multiple sclerosis while reigniting his artistic career is nothing short of inspiring.

His journey, from temporarily losing his vision to regaining his artistic confidence with the support of his friend, is a testament to resilience. His experiences with MS, and the challenges it brought to his creative process, have shaped not only his art but also his outlook on life. His return to art has become a source of inspiration for others facing similar challenges.

In featuring artists like Donald, *Emmett Magazine* aims to inspire its readers to embrace their obstacles, whether physical, emotional, or creative, and turn them into opportunities for growth. Donald's story reminds us that art can be a powerful vehicle for overcoming adversity, a message that resonates deeply with the magazine's readers.

As Donald continues to explore his creative path, his work stands as a beacon of perseverance and the power of art to transcend personal limitations. The quality of his art, combined with the depth of his personal story, makes him a compelling artist to watch in the coming years.

Follow Donald Partlow's Artistic Journey:

- Instagram: [@dpartlow2](https://www.instagram.com/dpartlow2)

- Featured in *Emmett Magazine* (available on Amazon and Barnes & Noble)

- Exhibiting at "Pieces of Me" solo exhibition, October 2024.

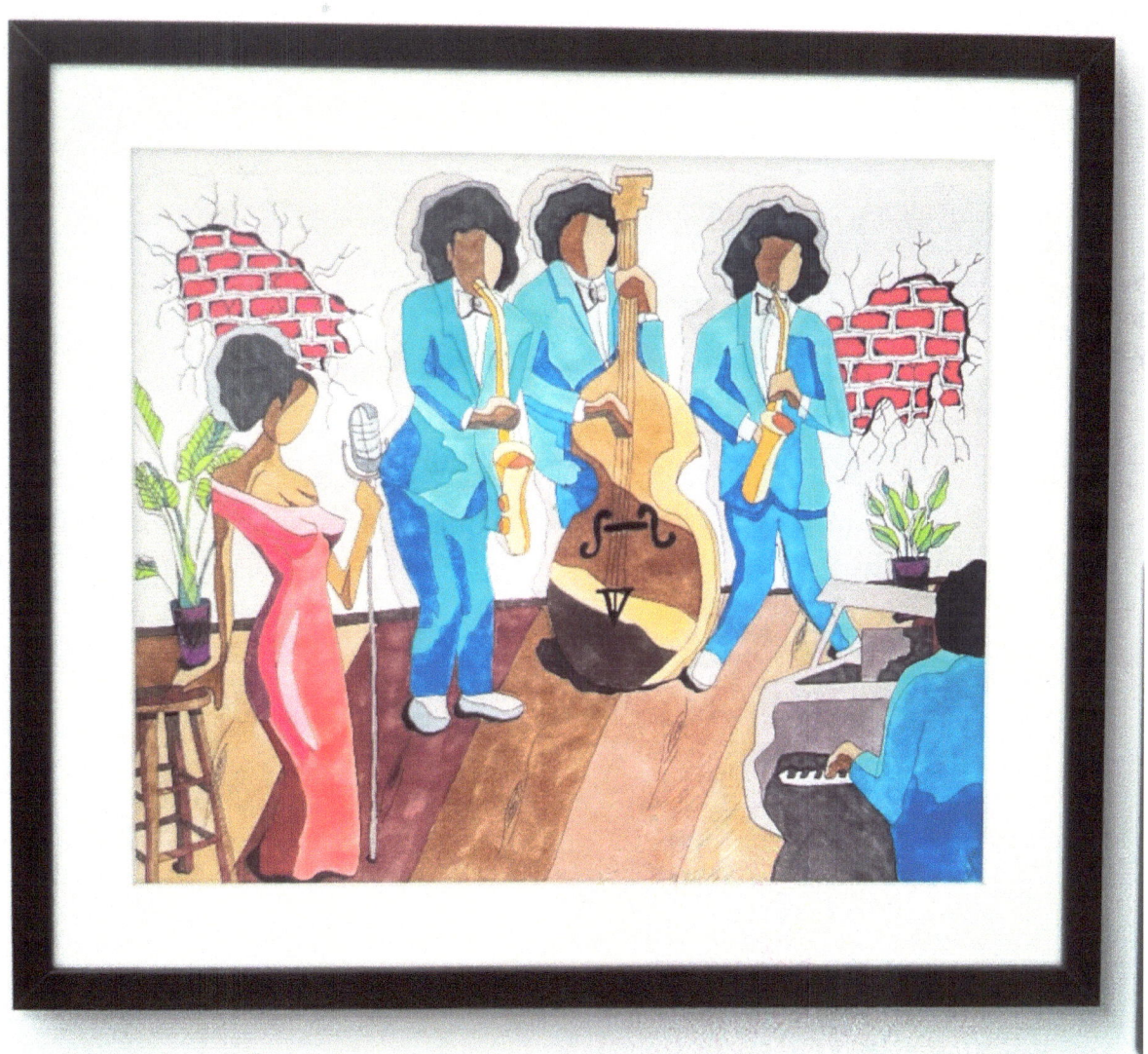

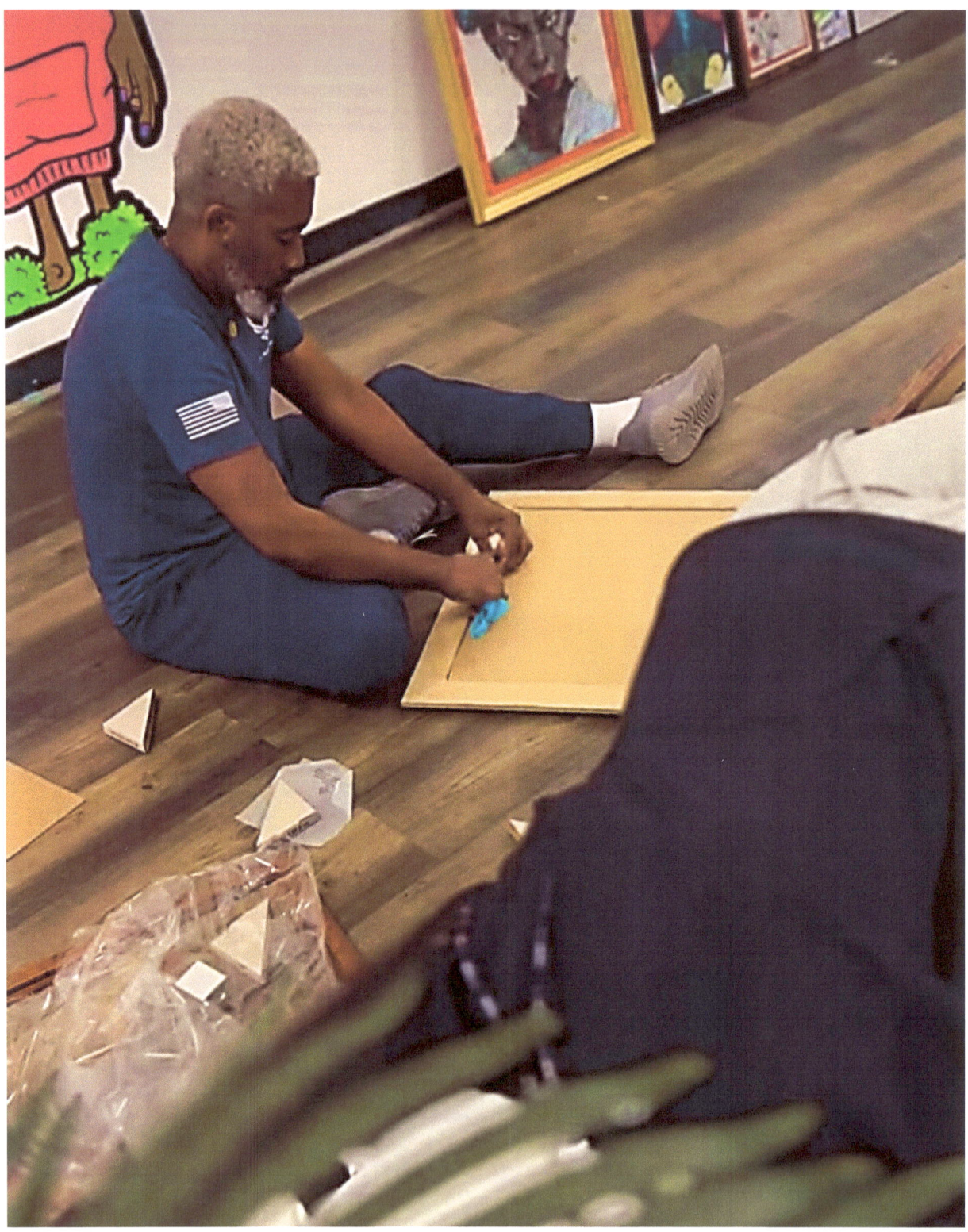

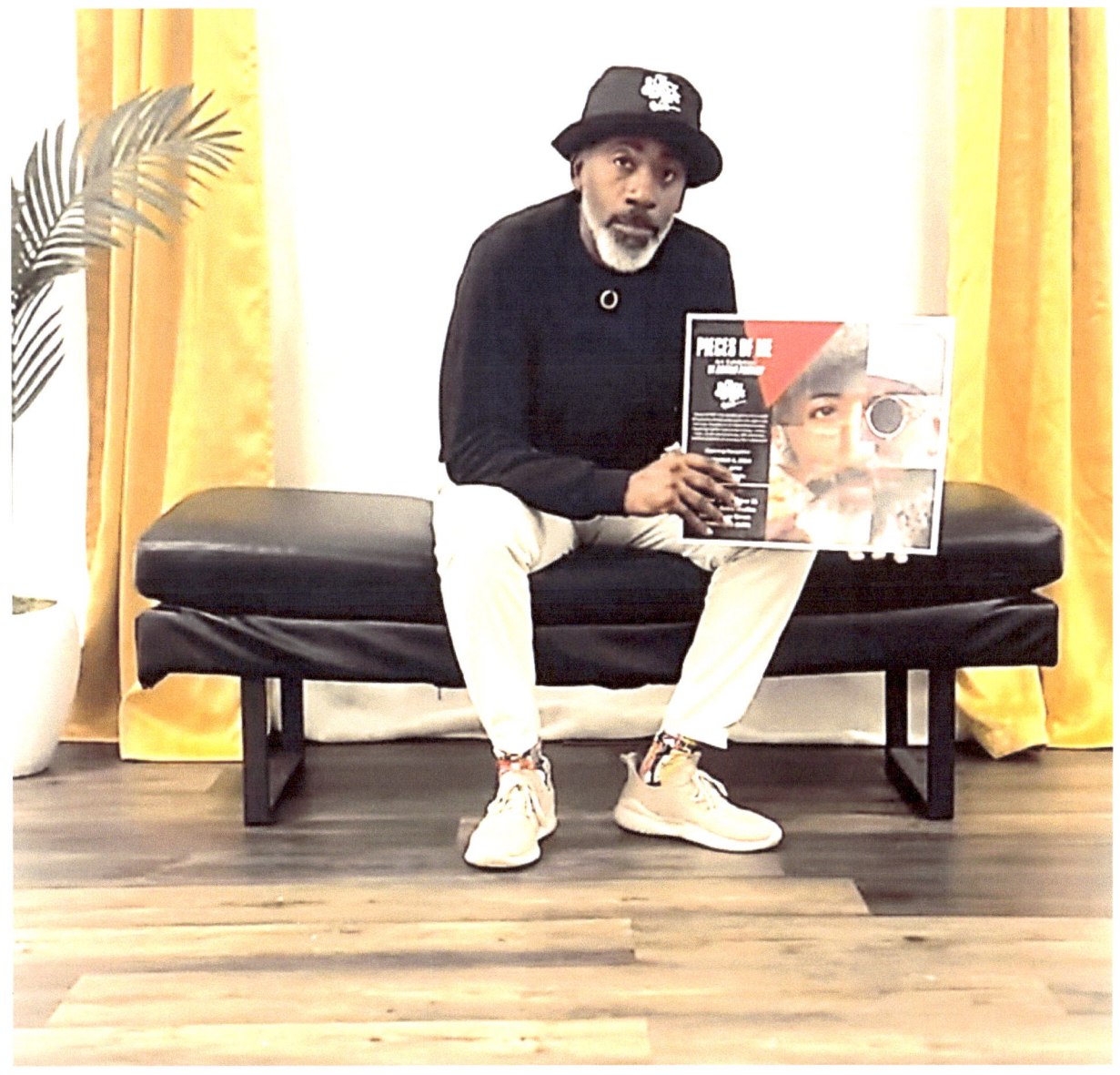

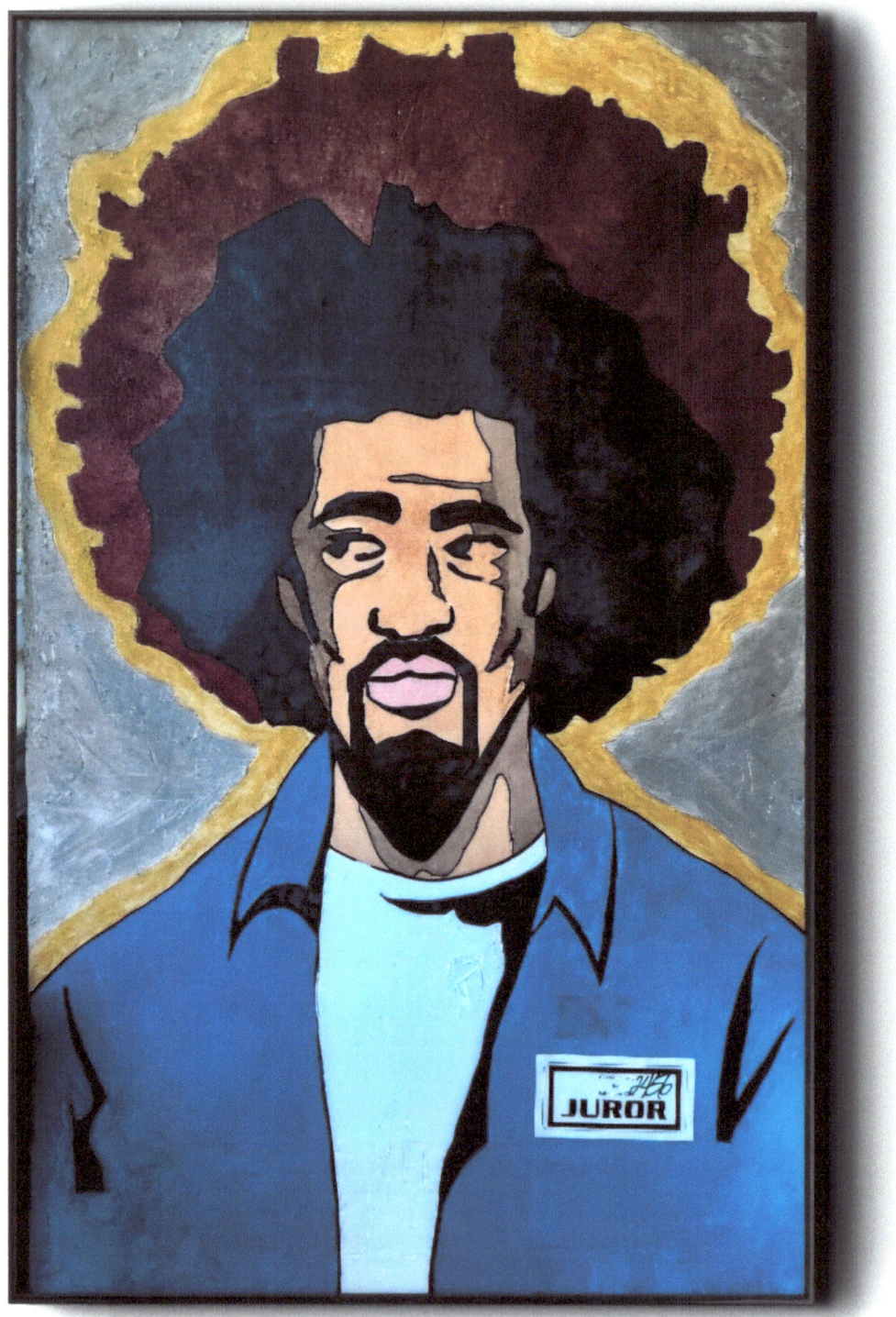

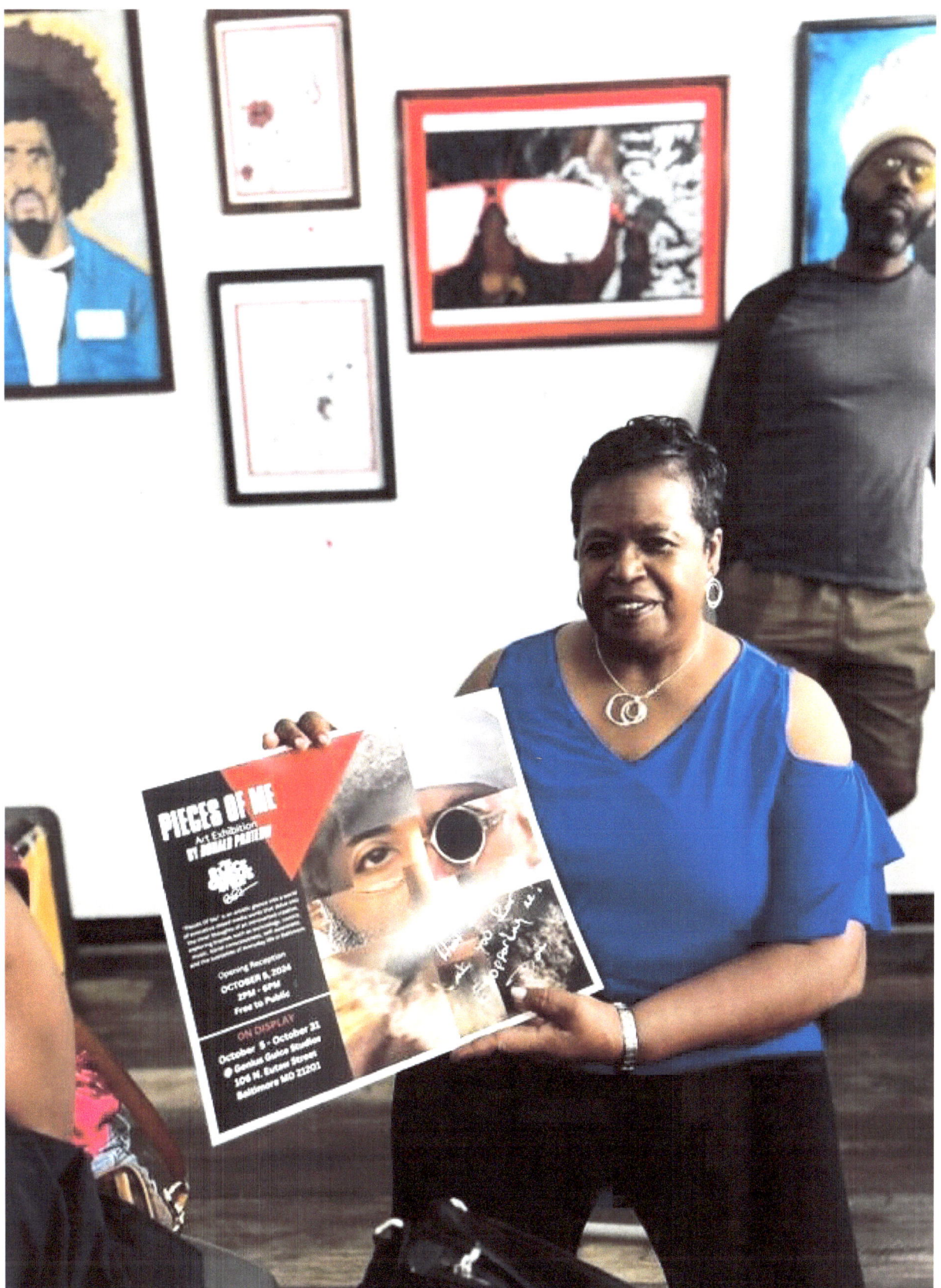

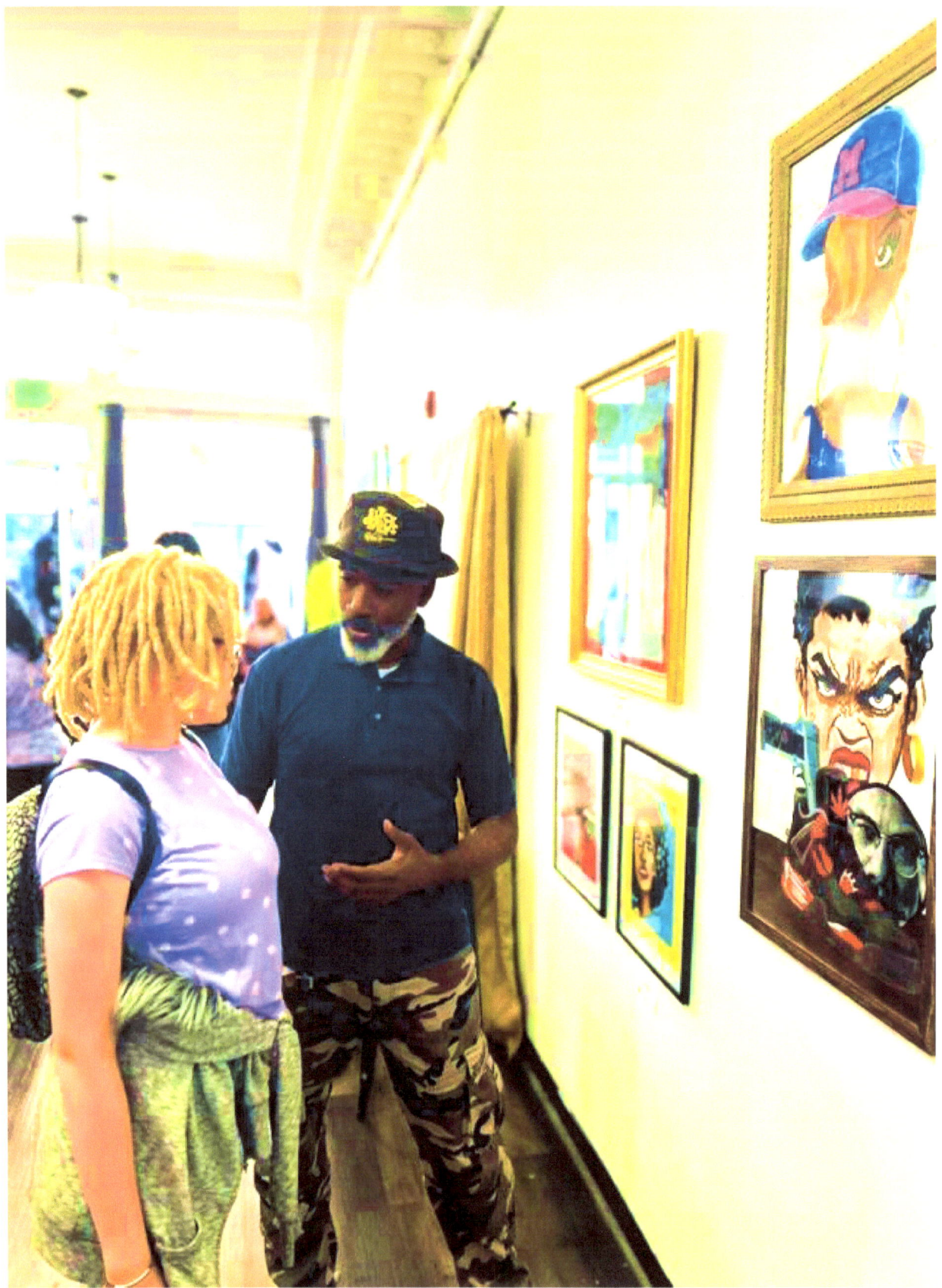

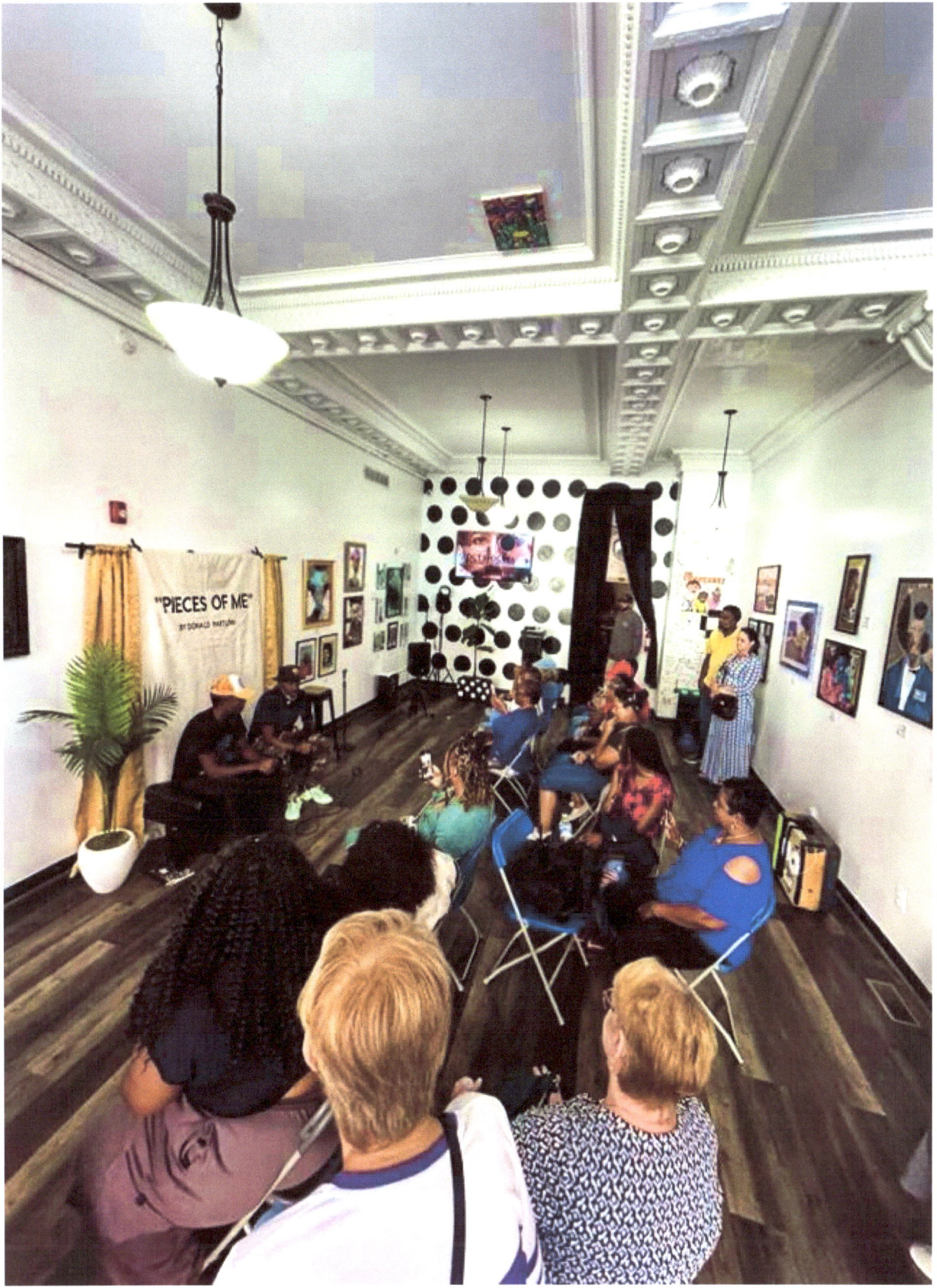

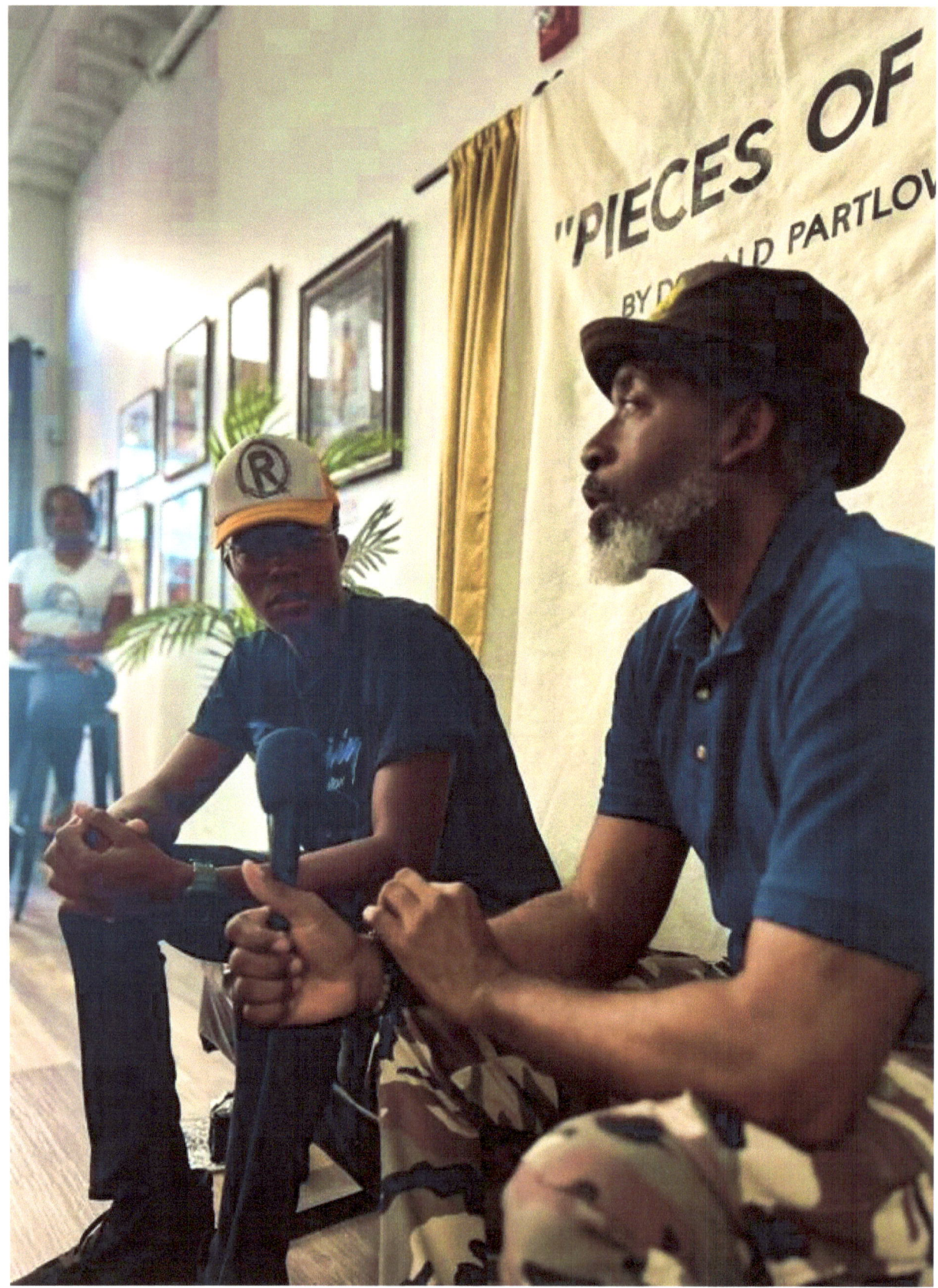

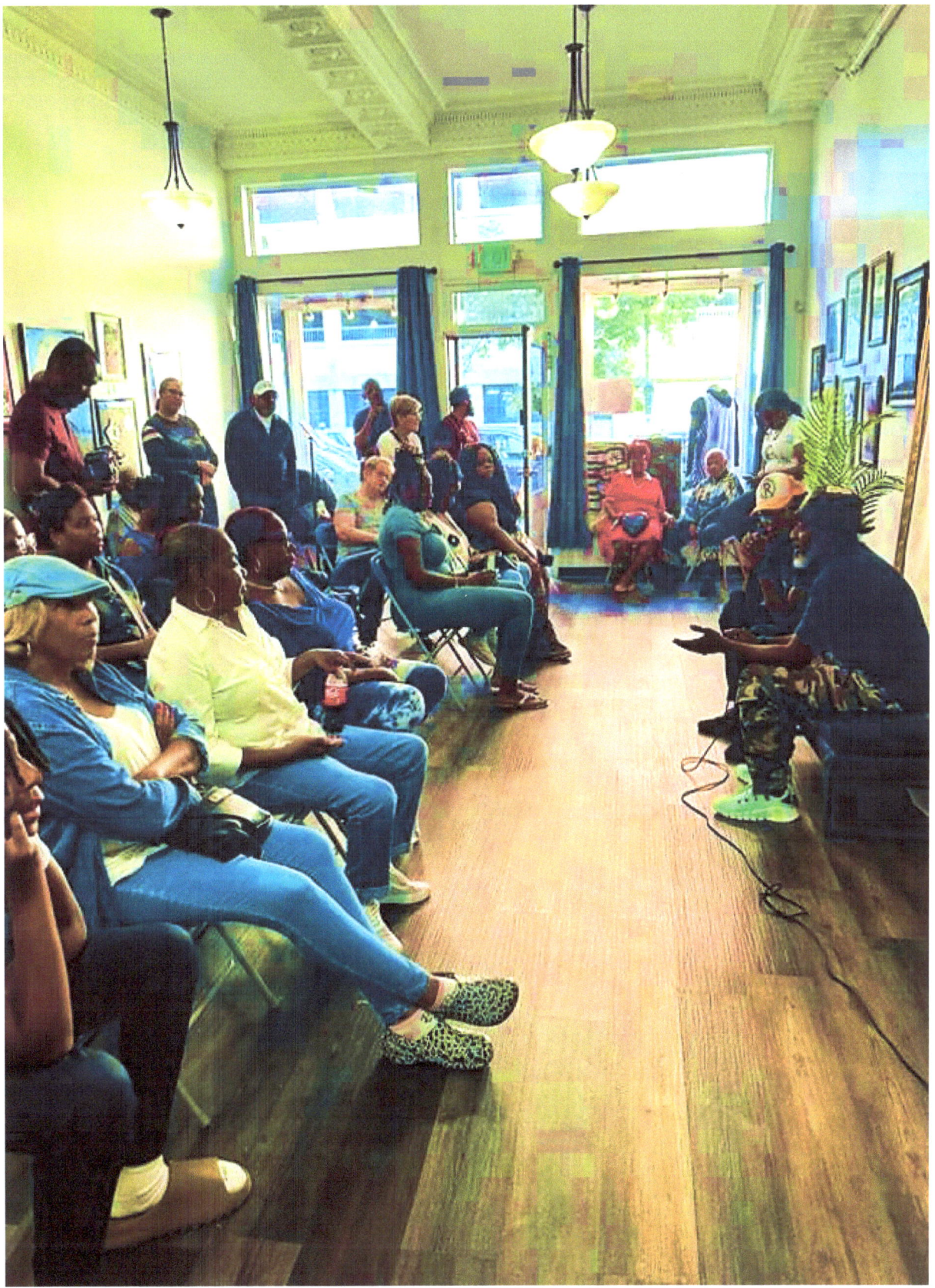

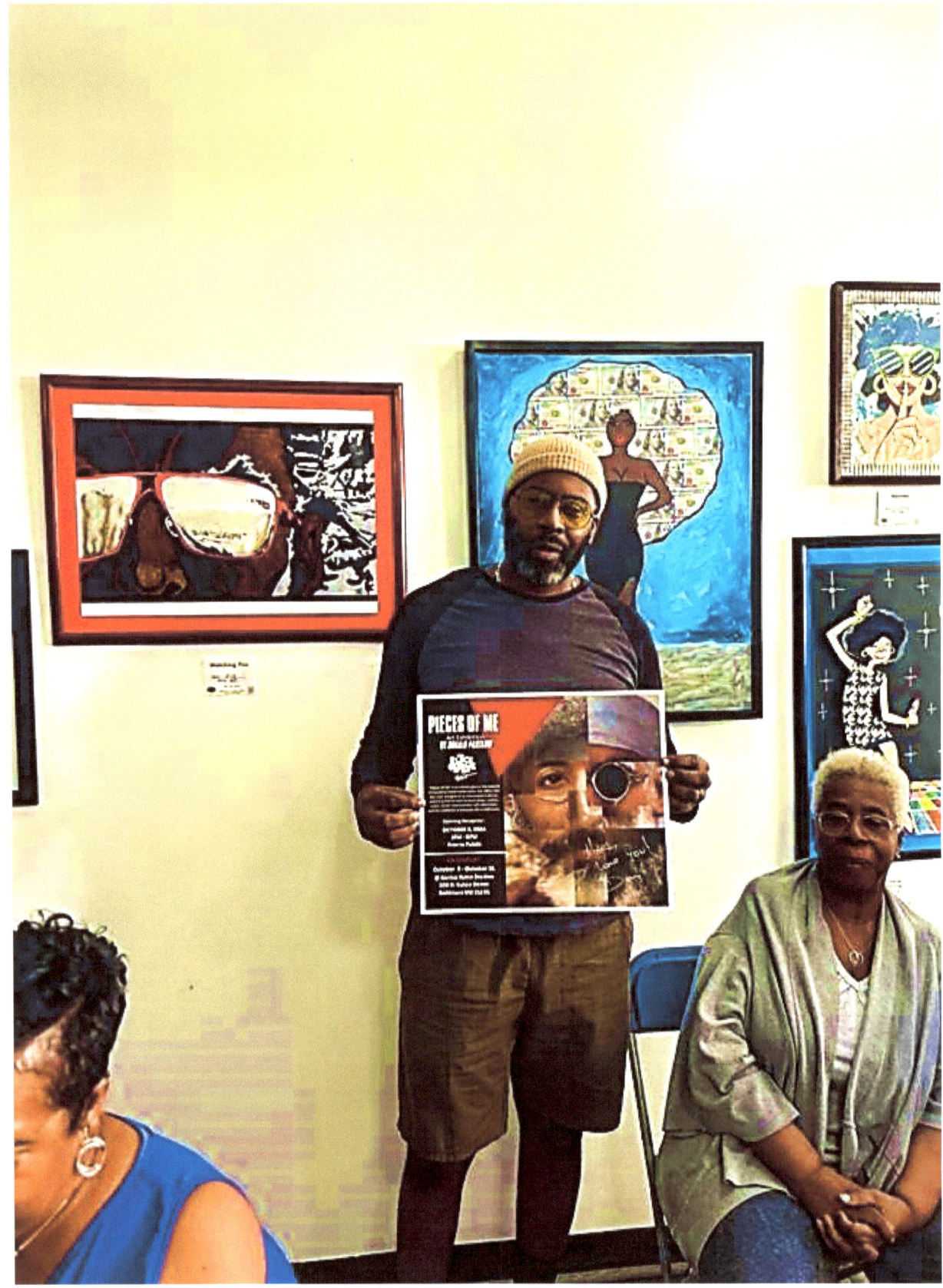

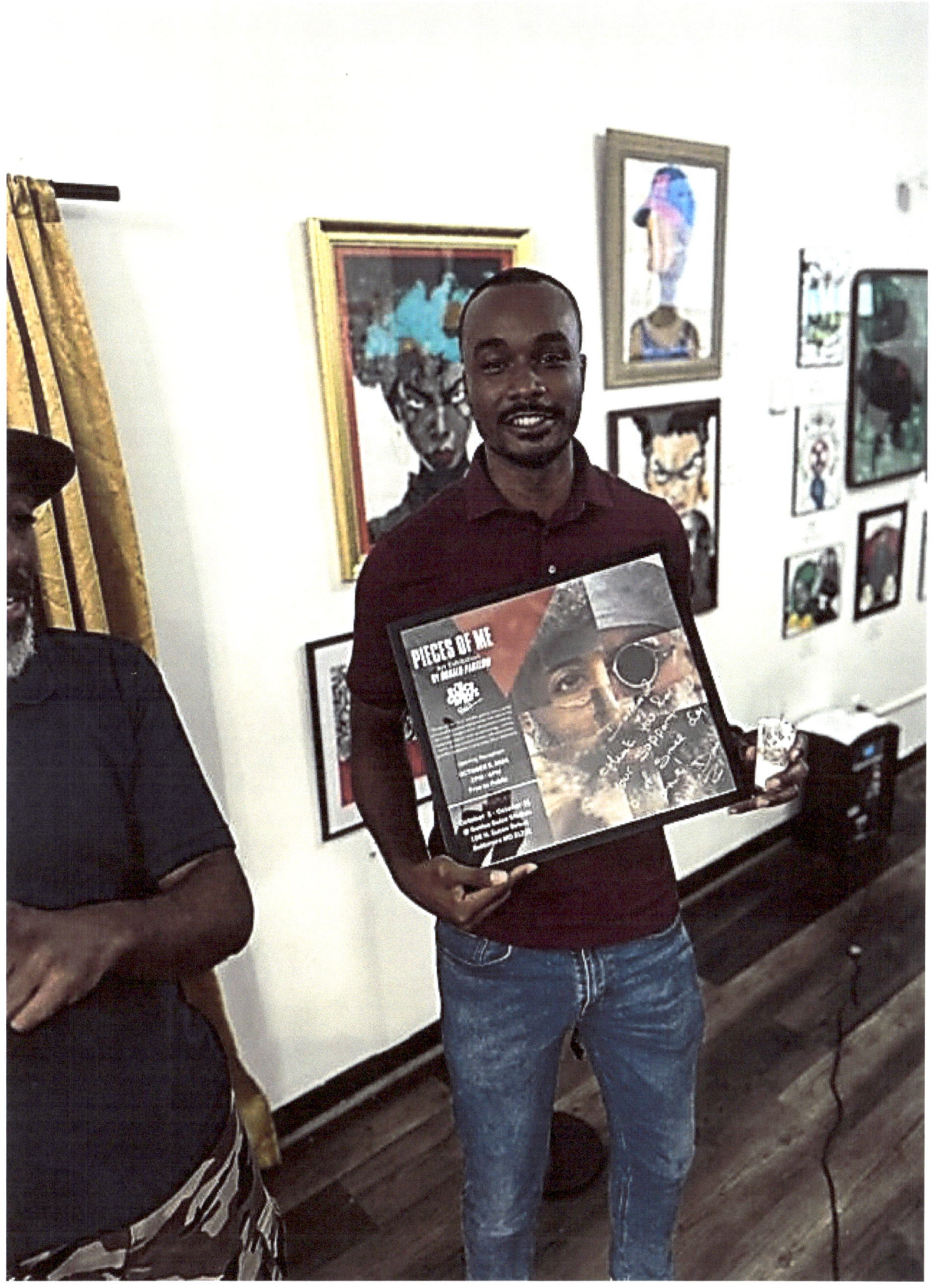

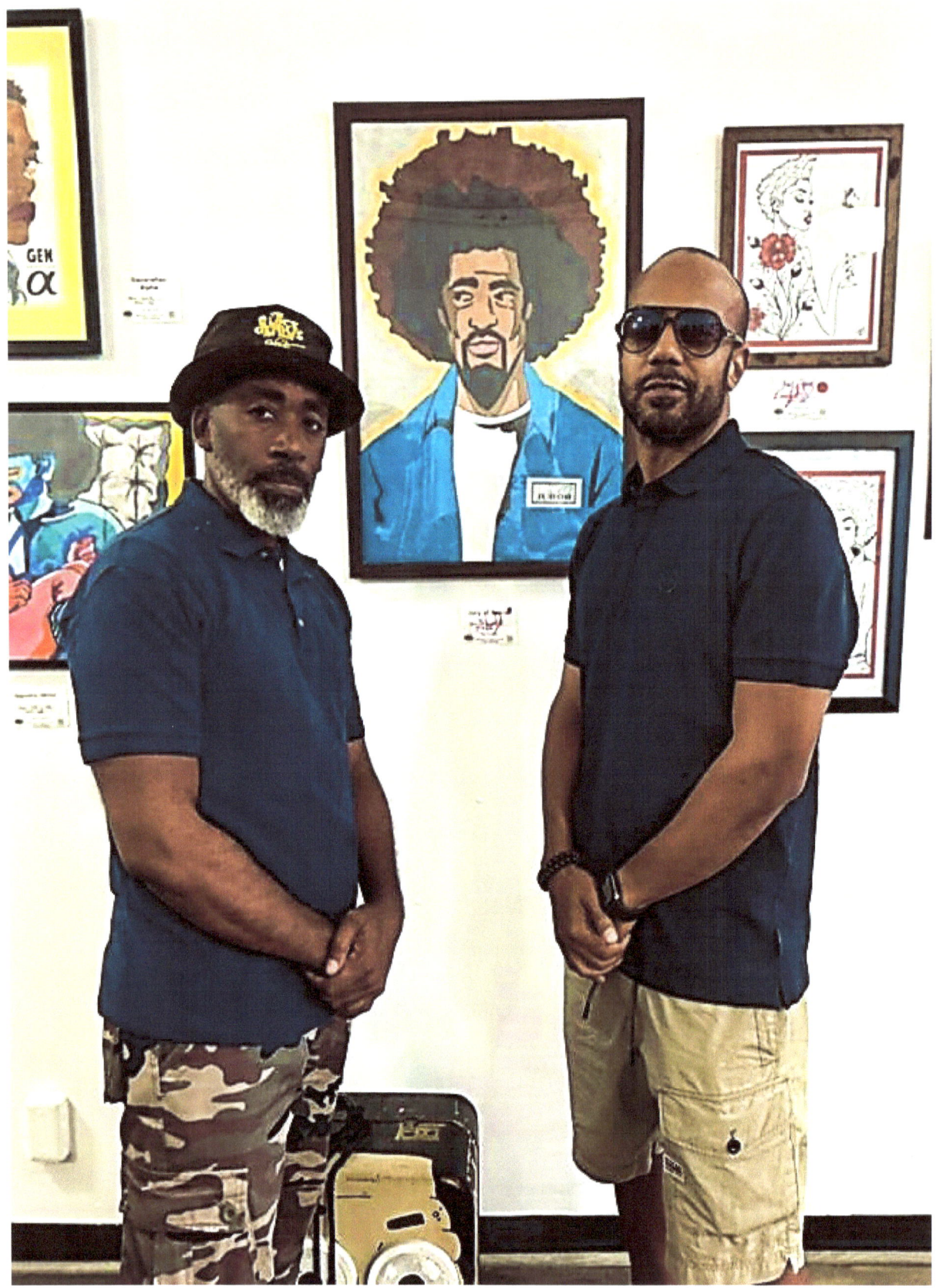

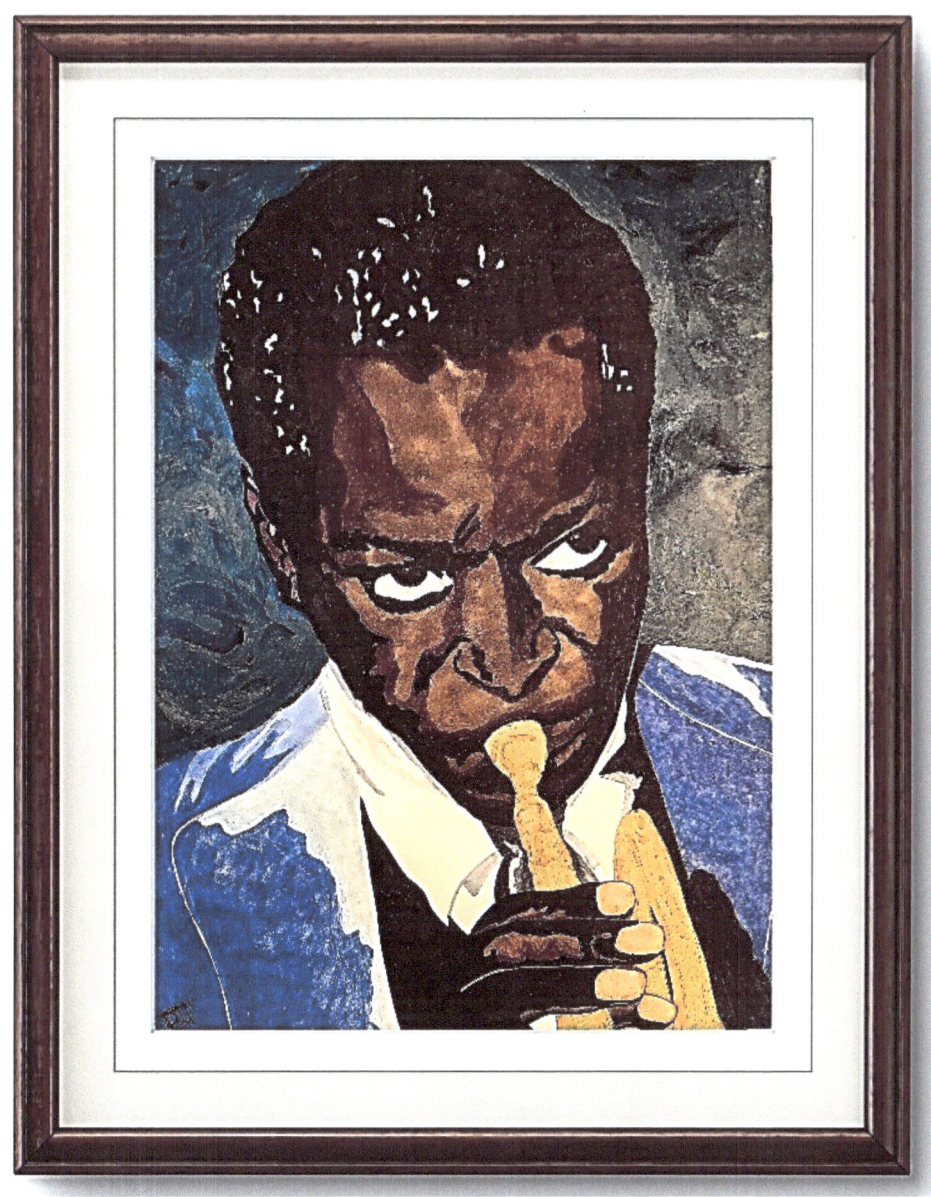

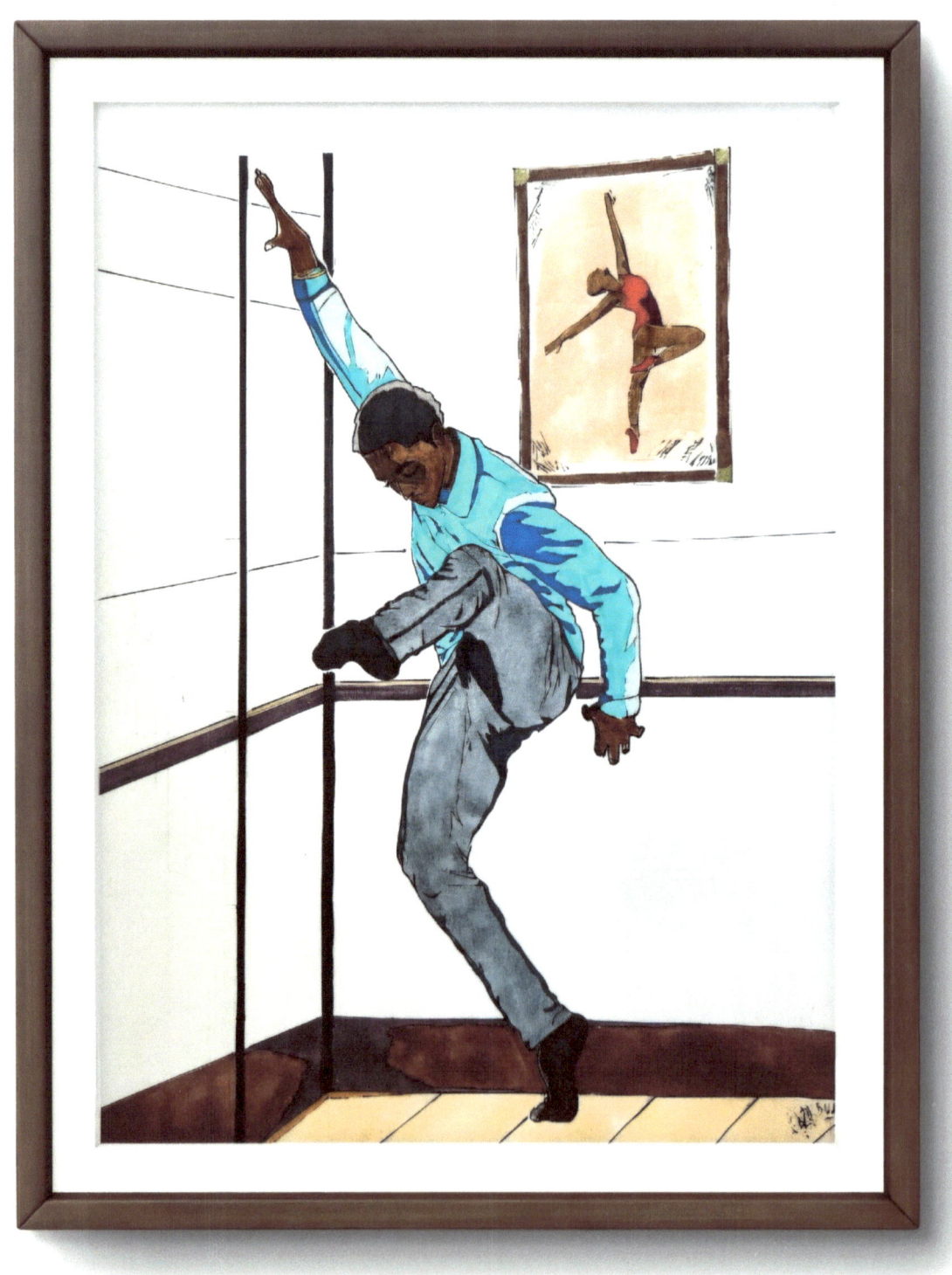

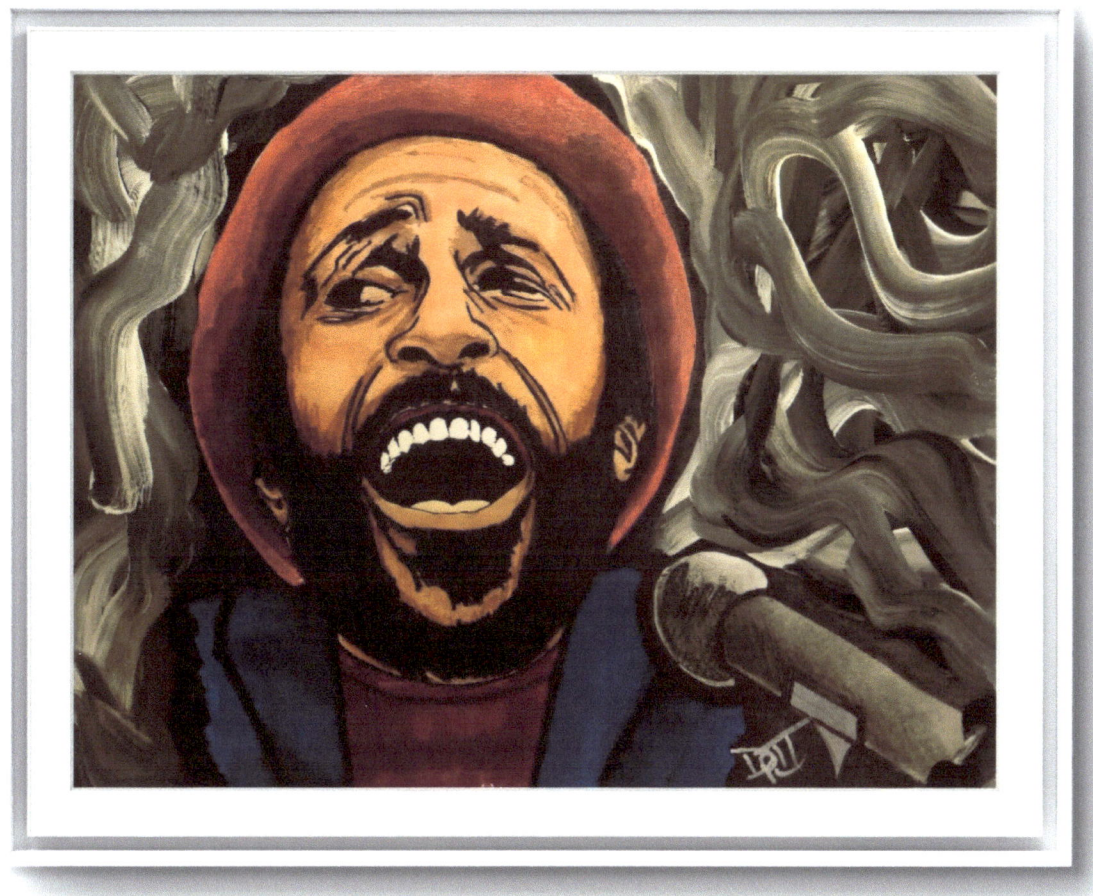

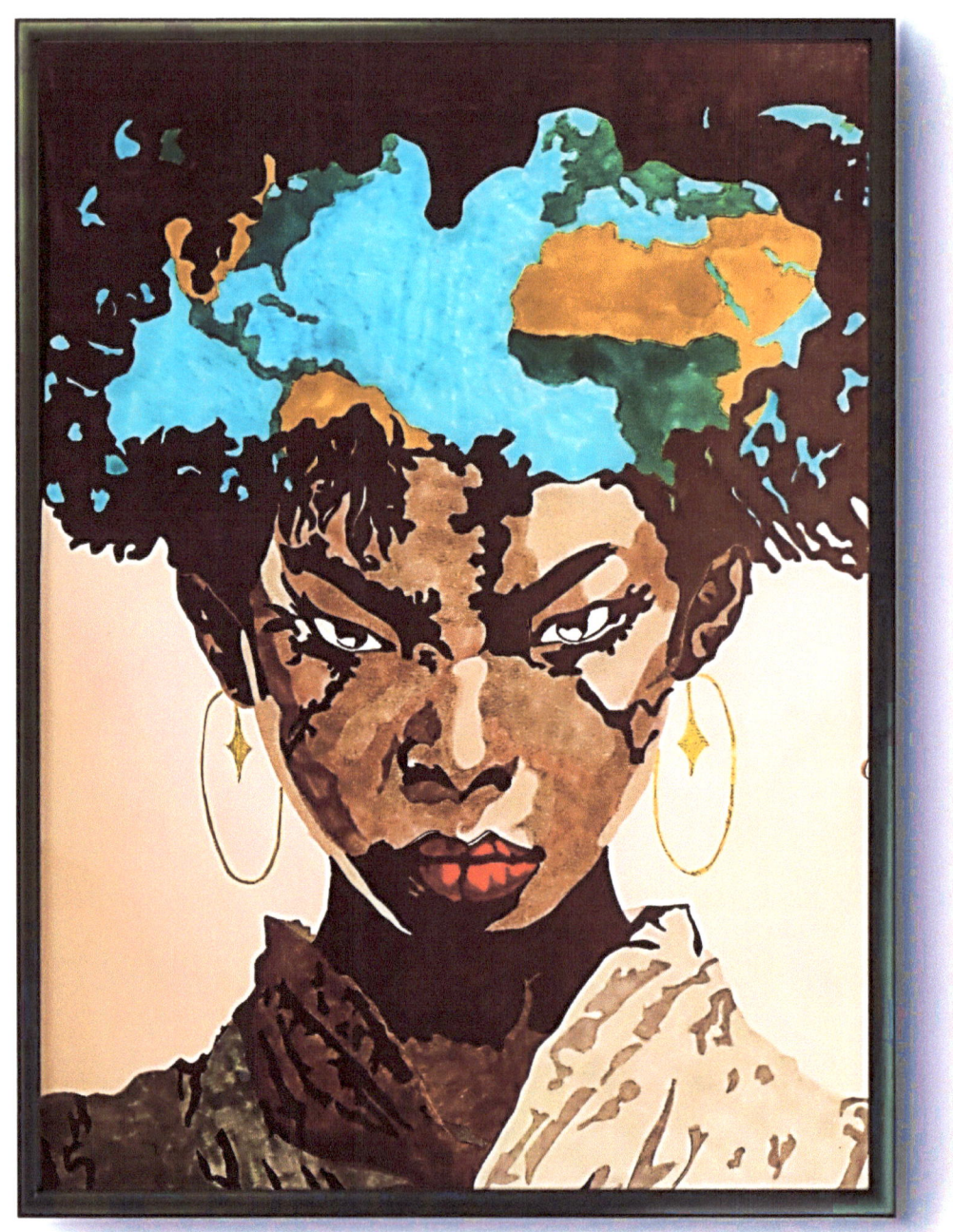

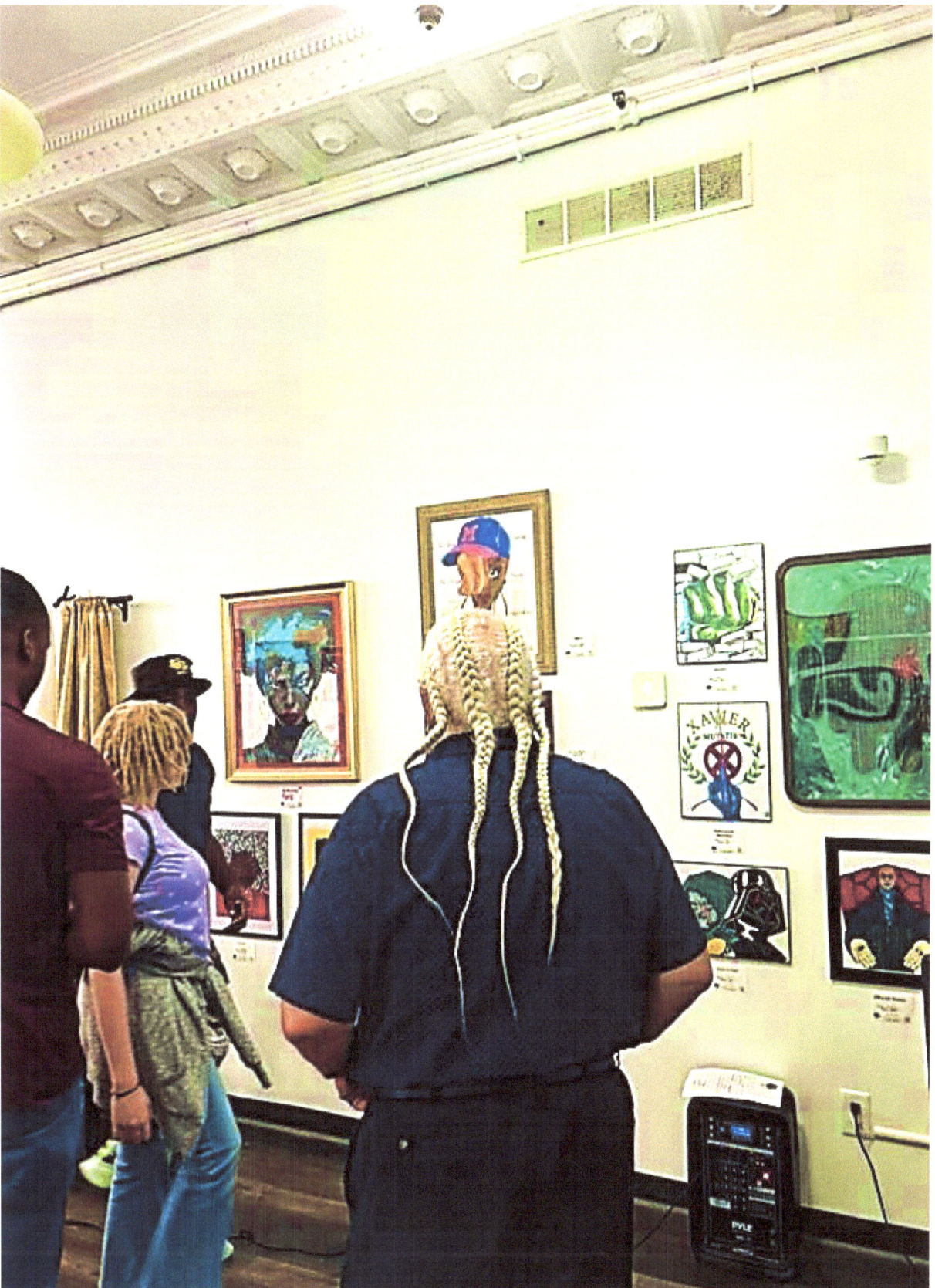

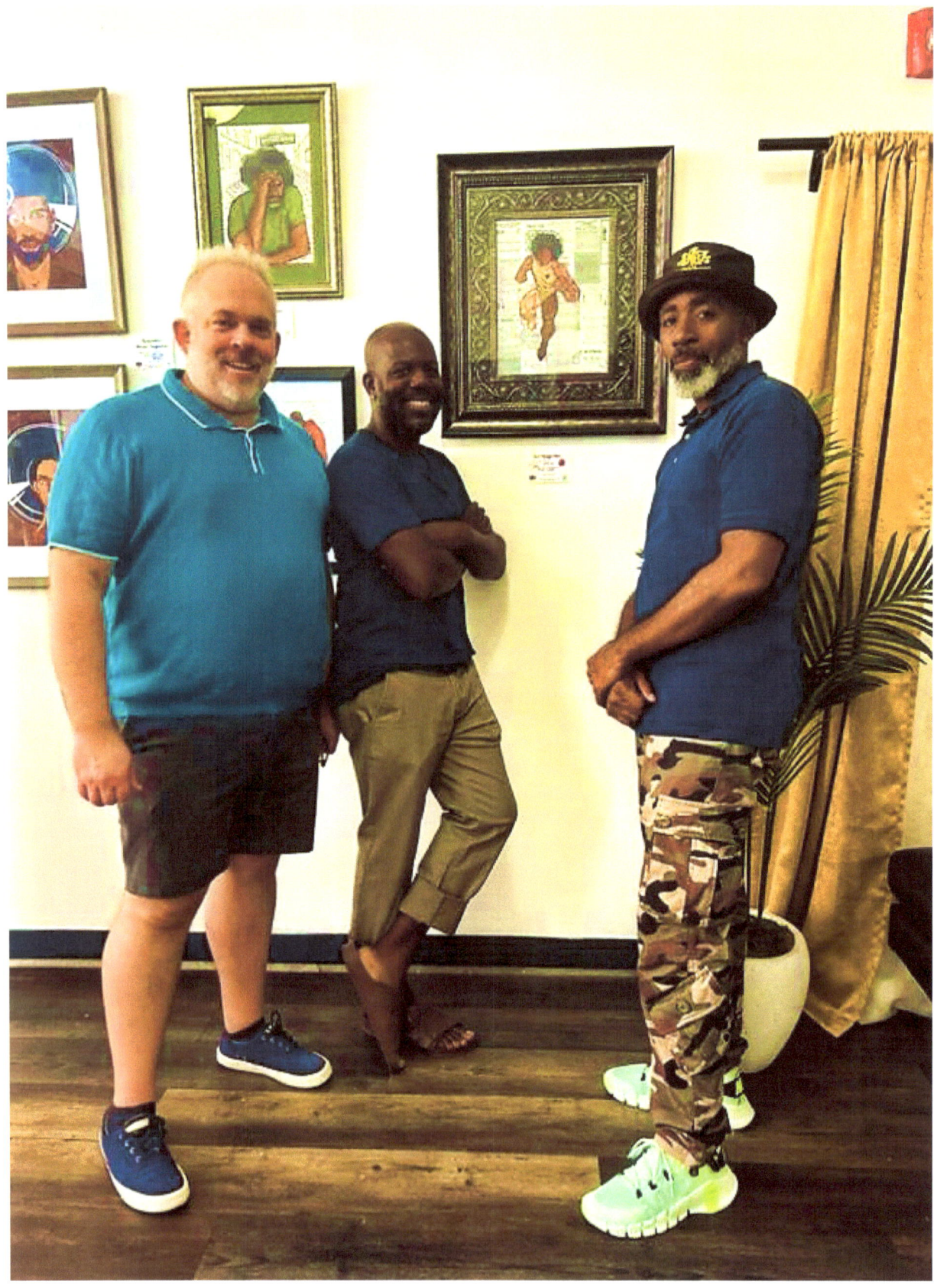

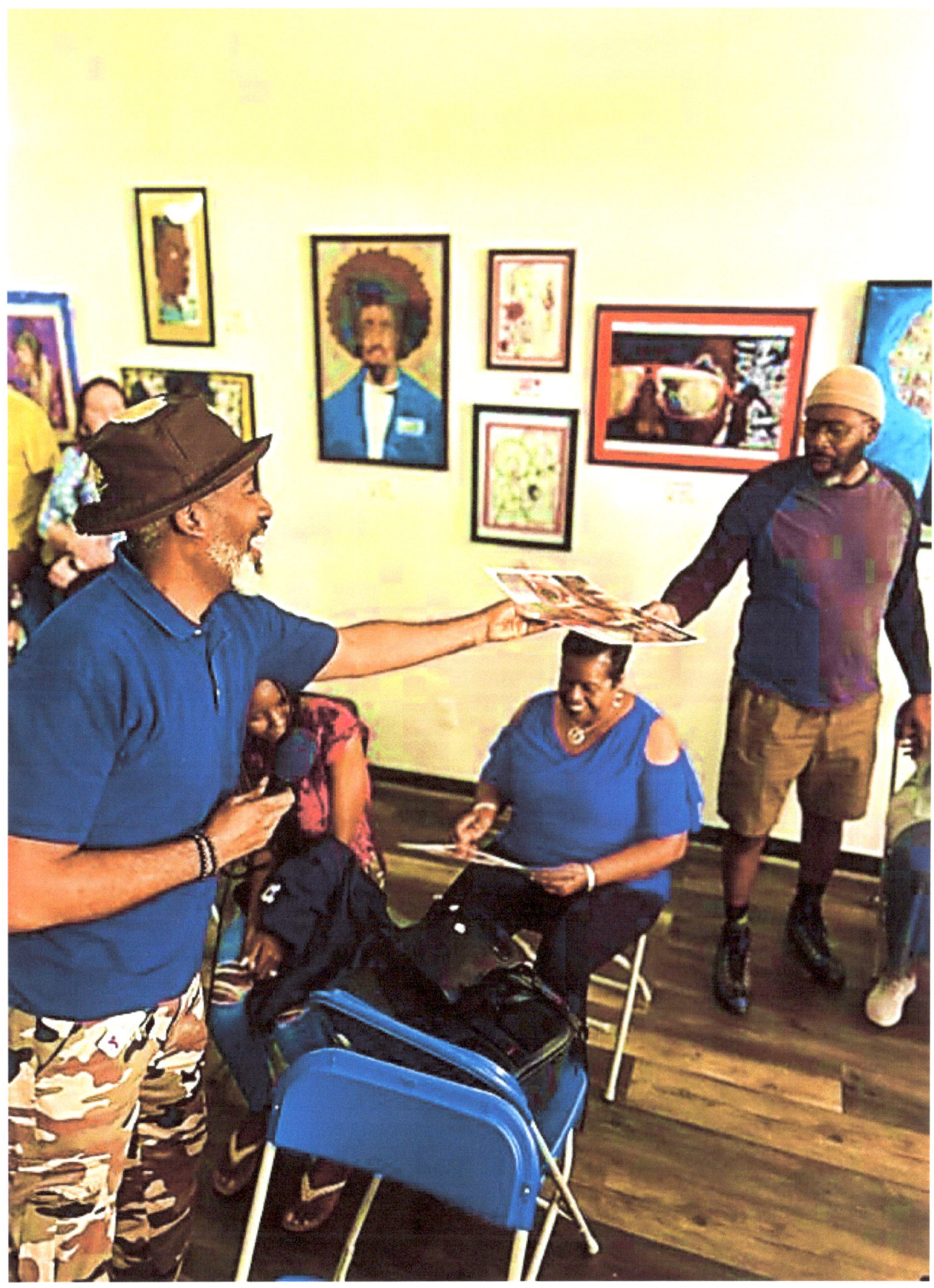

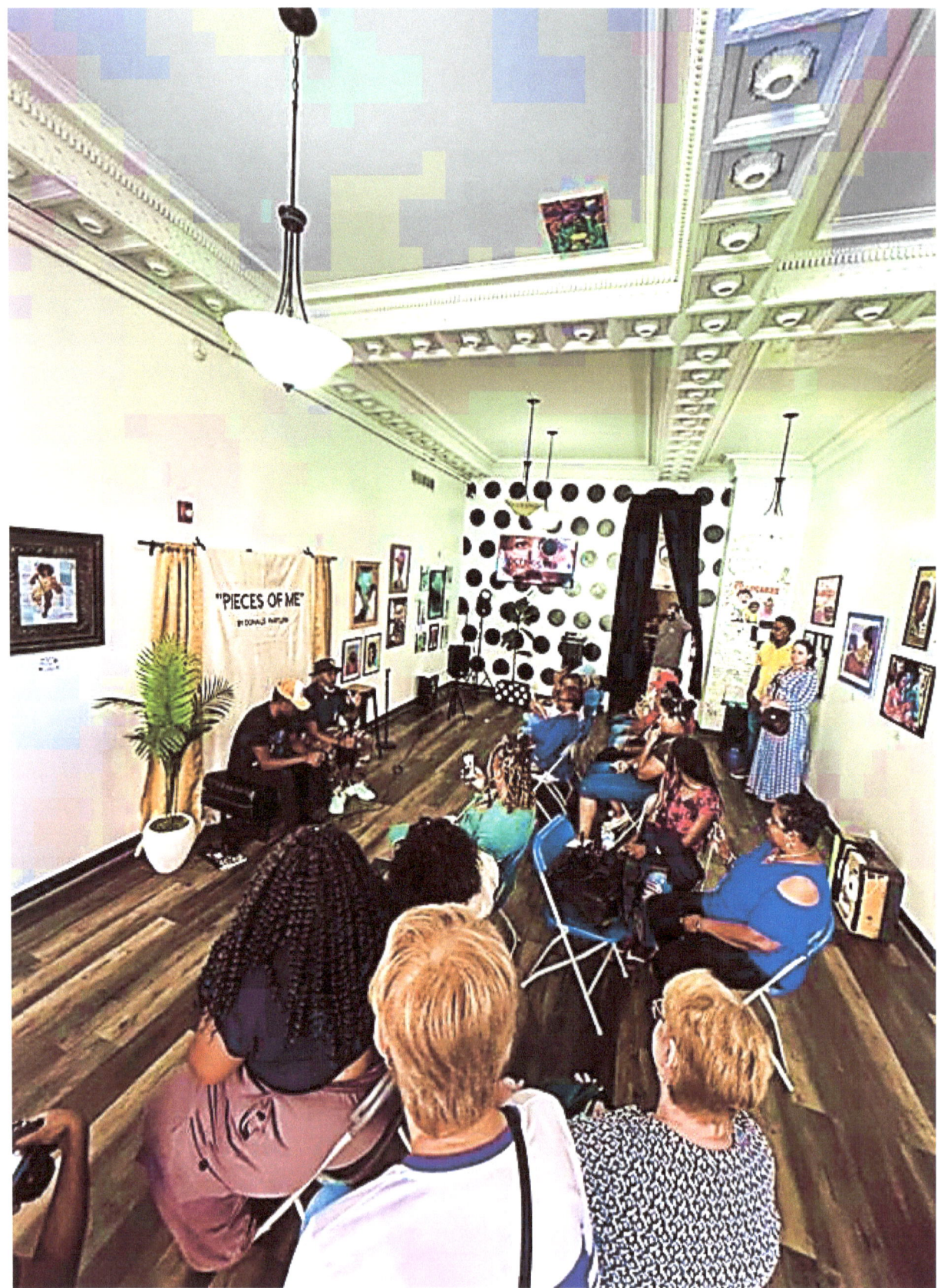

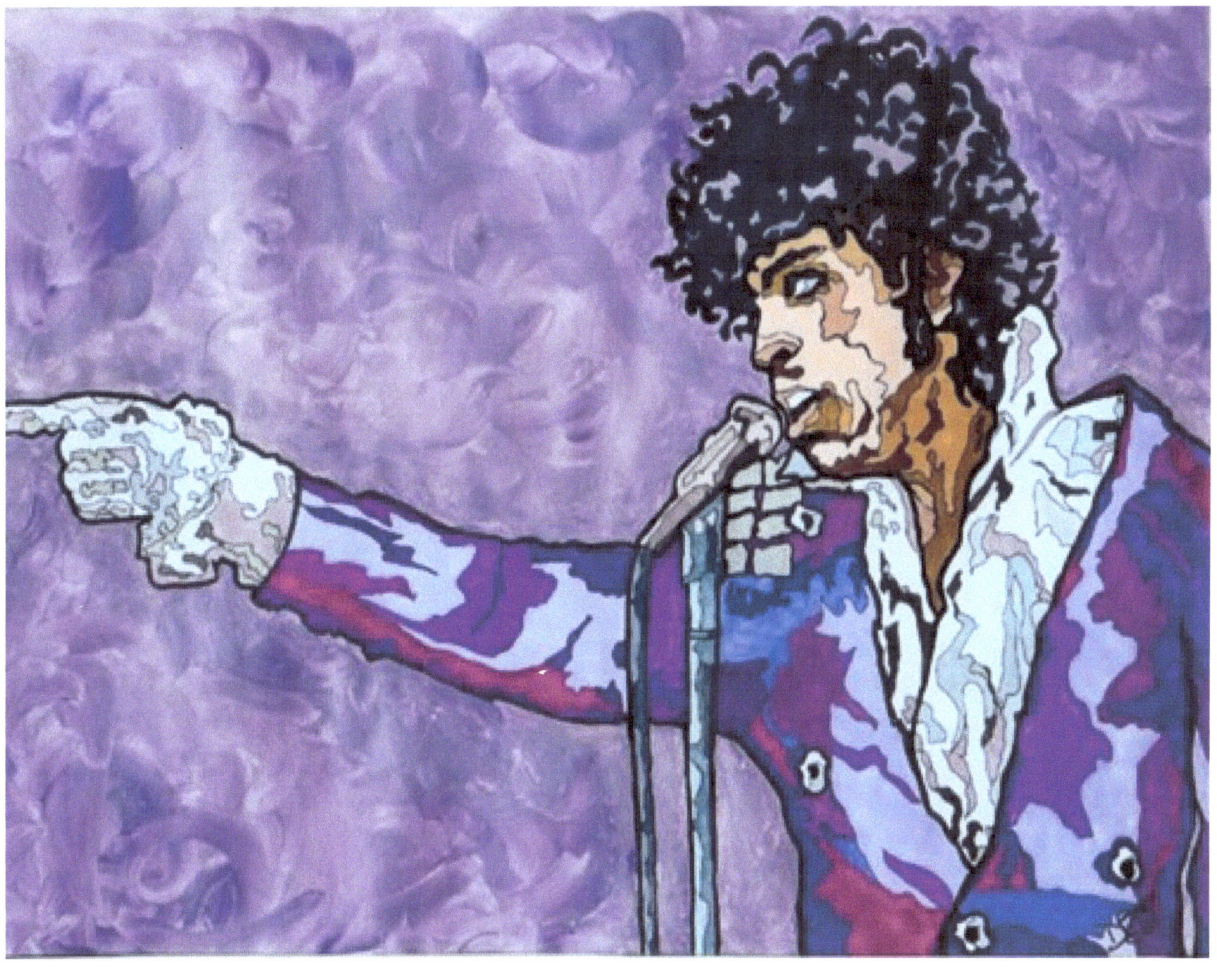

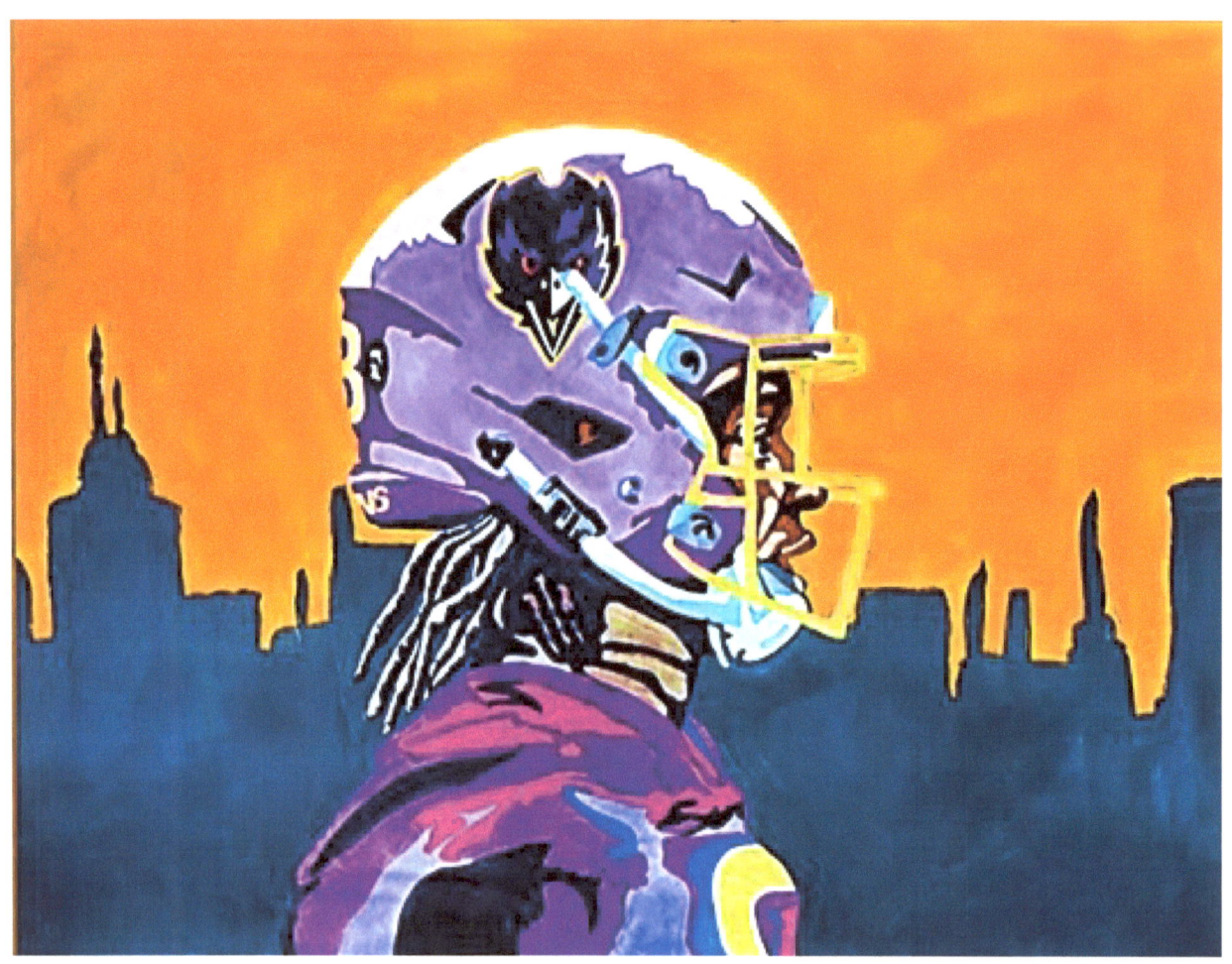

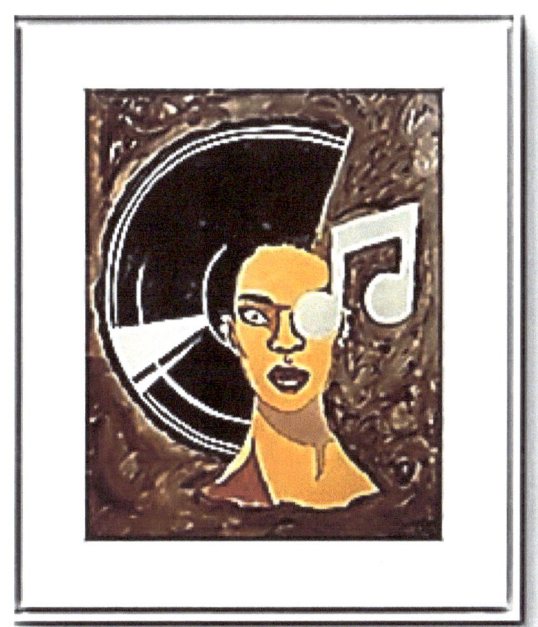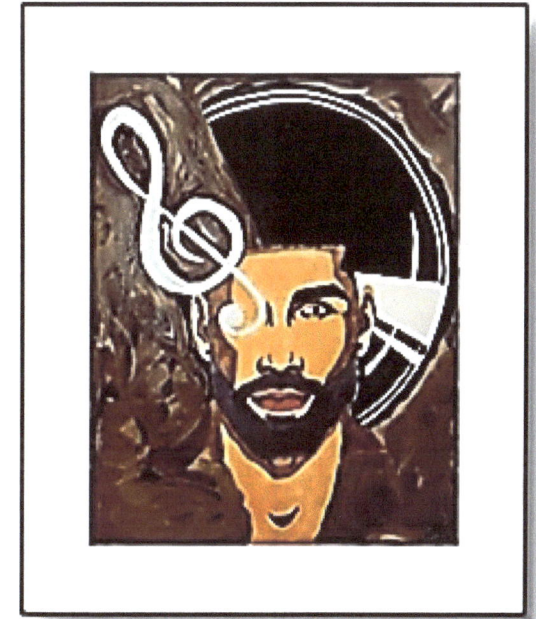

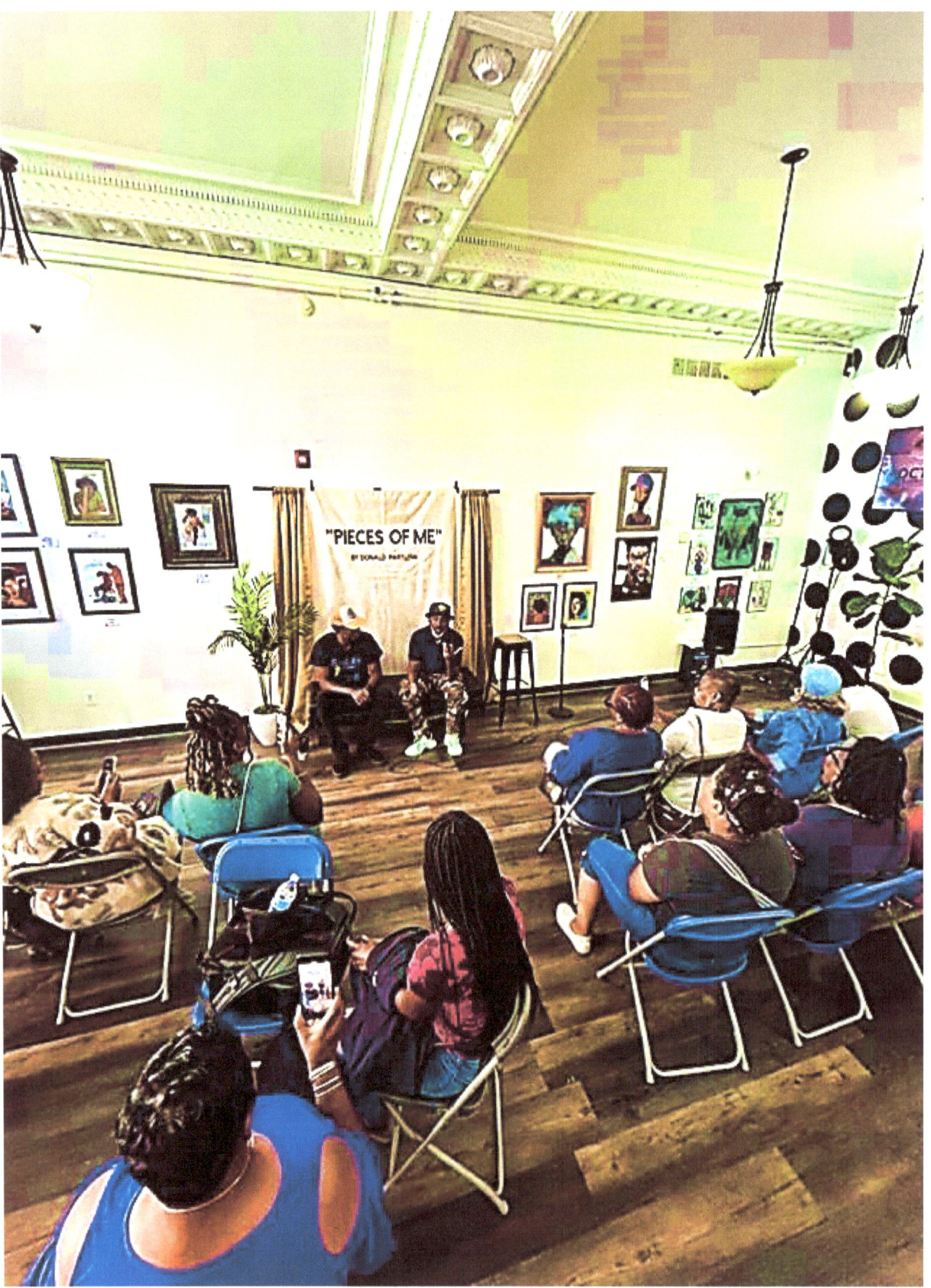

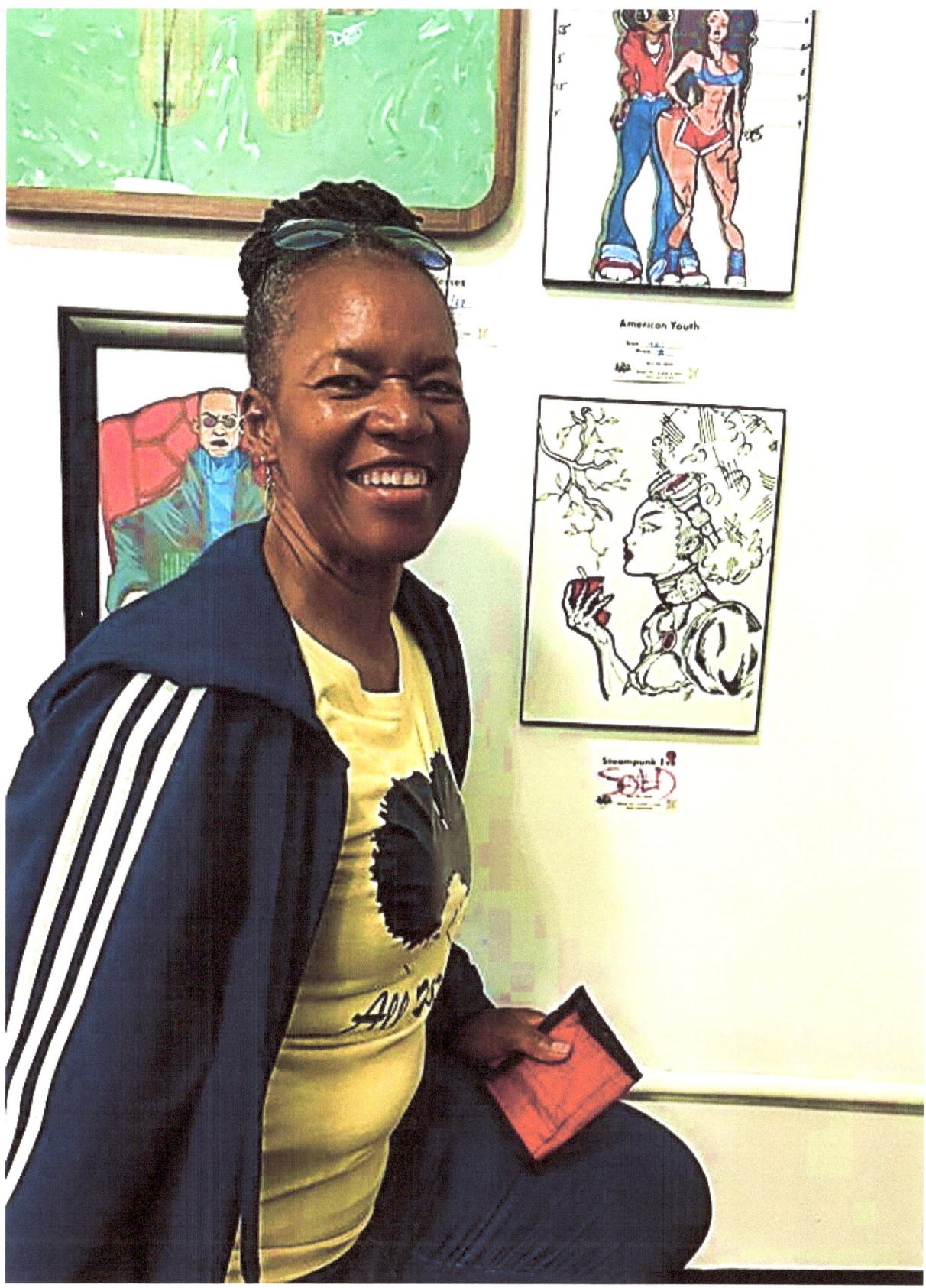

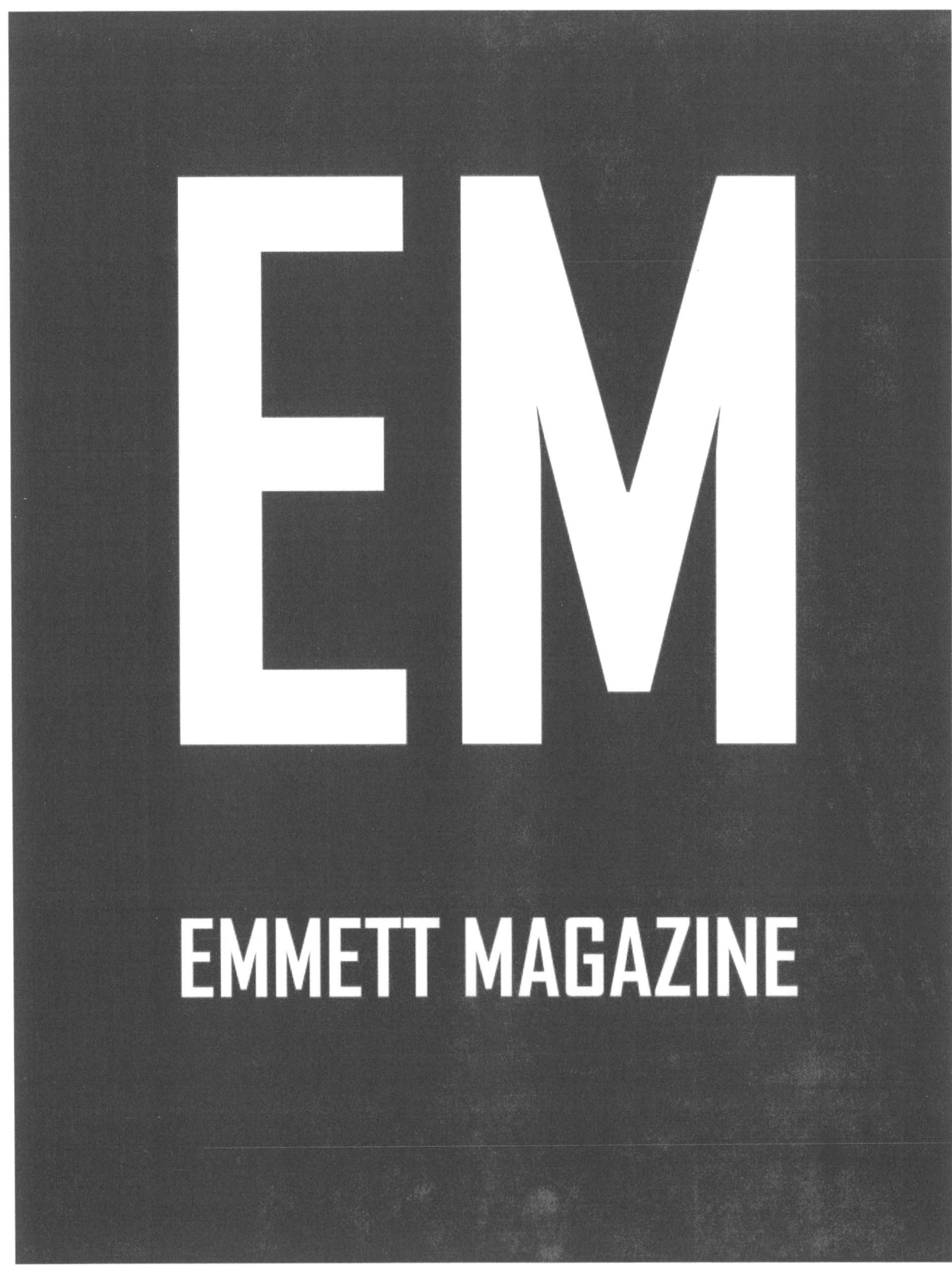